Prayers for Passing Years
SUSAN SAYERS

Milestones

GW00708284

Kevin
Mayhew

First published in 1996 by
KEVIN MAYHEW LTD
Rattlesden
Bury St Edmunds
Suffolk IP30 0SZ

ISBN 0 86209 833 5
Catalogue No 1500071

0 1 2 3 4 5 6 7 8 9

Cover photograph courtesy of Pictor International

Design by Veronica Ward
Artwork by Graham Johnstone

Edited by Peter Dainty
Typesetting by Louise Hill
Printed and bound in Great Britain

CONTENTS

DEDICATION

O God, lead me on
   from where I am
   to where you
   would have me be.

Give me the patience
   to accept the bits
   I'd rather do without
   and courage to move
   when you beckon.

Into your hands, O Lord,
    I commit my spirit.

I commit the good
    I have tried to do,
    and the good I have avoided.

I commit my heart
    with all the love
    that you find inside.

I commit my living
    and my dying
    into your safe keeping
    for ever.

NEEDING GOD

It's been a long time
   since I spoke with you.
Do you remember
   who I am?
So much else
   has crowded in
   that I haven't found time
   to pray.

The trouble is,
   as I've started to realise,
   I needed you
   all the time I crowded you out.

It felt awkward
   and embarrassing
   to make that first move back,
   but already
   I sense the beauty of your peace
   washing around me.

Forgive me, Lord.
Your welcome
   fills my eyes and my heart with tears.

Hold me close to you,
   Lord, my God,
   my shepherd.

A lot of me
   wants to go racing off
   to the thickets and cliffs
   away from your care.

Hold me close
   and let me know
   your presence
   whispering courage
   and strength
   until the desire to wander away
   wanders away.

Where are you, O God?
I search for you
   and long to feel you near,
   but my prayers
   hang in the empty air
   and I have to force myself
   to bother,
   as I feel nothing.

All I hang on to
   is that feelings
   are not everything,
   and just because this fog
   surrounds me
   does not mean
   that everything has gone.

One thing I have discovered –
   I had not realised before
   how much I delighted
   in your company.

GOD'S HELP

I want to thank you,
    Lord God of my hope,
    for rescuing me from despair.

It is true
    that you haul us
    out of swampy ground
    and set our feet on rock.

I was sinking
    and close to giving up.
Too many sorrows,
    too much pain
    and utter weariness
    engulfed me.

And there were the strong arms
    of your reassuring presence;
    there was the practical help
    through the hands of your friends.

Extraordinary as it may seem,
    I feel quite different.
Safe.

Loving God,
    your caring
    over the last few months
    has amazed me.

I had heard it said
    that when one door closed
    another opened;
    but I was sceptical.

And that door
    was slammed so suddenly.

The strange thing is,
    I had hardly noticed
    the new door opening
    until I was halfway through.

Thank you,
    my loving God
    for your providing.

GOD'S GUIDANCE

God of wisdom,
  I need your help.

It is as if I am standing
  at a crossroads,
  with signs pointing
  in different directions
  and I need
  to make a choice.

As I weigh up
  the advantages and disadvantages
  of each direction
  I ask you to guide me
  and cause me to bring to mind
  everything necessary
  to making
  the best decision.

Lord, after crawling
   through traffic jams
   and feeling the world was jammed,
   we got to the airport
   and took to the air.

And suddenly the
   congested roads
   were back in proportion –
   tiny ribbons woven
   through open green hills.

And I thought of the way
   your over-all vision
   is so badly needed
   when our lives get jammed,
   to help us get things
   back in proportion again.

GOD'S REFRESHMENT

Fill me again
   with your Spirit, O God.

Spread through my mind
   until I think your way.

Wander through my emotions
   and bring them in line
   with the measure of your love.

Anoint my wounds
   with the balm of your healing.

Empower my being
   to reflect your beauty
   in the way I live,
   from now onwards
   to the end of my days.

After the turmoil,
    God of peace,
    you bring me to this
    quiet haven for a while.

I am so grateful
    for a breathing space,
    for respite,
    for refreshment.

I remember the words
    of the psalm –
    'He leads me beside still waters' –
    and know them to be true.

The peace is filtering
    deeper and deeper
    into my being
    and in the tranquillity
    I know
    that you are God.

Holy God
   the radiance of your love
   touches my life
   with tenderness
   and warmth.

It stretches out the doubts
   and calms them.

It searches out the misgivings
   and reassures
It mops up errors,
   binds unravelled relationships
   and pierces prejudice.

Holy God
   wrap your radiance
   around my life
   until my life
   is hidden in yours.

MAKING PROGRESS

How odd it is, Lord,
   that so often
   it's the times we feel
   we're getting nowhere
   that turn out to be
   times of surging growth!

And I suspect
   the reverse is true as well.

Next time I'm hanging on
   for dear life, Lord,
   remind me
   that spiritual progress
   can go on in tunnels
   as well as in open country.

This journey through life
    goes round in circles
    sometimes, Lord.

Same old sins;
    same old weaknesses
    to overcome.

But perhaps
    it's more of a spiral
    than a circle.

Still revisiting
    the same places, it's true,
    but travelling deeper,
    edging down
    into the heart of God.

Hard Times

I would be a liar, Lord,
   if I pretended all was well.

And there's no fooling you,
   I know.

So let's be honest about this –
   the situation I am in
   hurts like hell.

I can't see anything
   good in it at all.

All I know is that
   you are a good God –
   the Good God –
   and I offer you
   these broken fragments of praise.

It is difficult not to feel hurt
    when you have been passed over
    and dismissed.

I know, Lord,
    that it's probably
    very good for my humility,
    and perhaps it draws attention
    to some empire building
    which needed to be checked.

But it still hurts.
Please help me to forgive,
    leaving no trace of resentment.

Help me to grow from this,
    and welcome it as
    a means of becoming
    closer to you.

Why is it, Lord,
  that you answered my prayer for patience
  with an increasingly irritating situation?

Could it be
  that you're giving me
  extra practice?

At first I resented this,
  but now, on thinking it over,
  I have to admit
  that it makes good sense.

All I ask is
  the odd break
  between rounds!

SPECIAL OCCASIONS

Lord God,
   this is an invitation.

I have been inviting all my loved ones
   to this celebration
   and you are the
   most important guest.

Bless our festivities
   and all the preparations
   so that our time together
   will be filled with joy
   in your presence.

We have made our vows
   in your presence, Lord,
   and laid down the single life
   to become this new creation –
   a married couple.

We invited you
   to the wedding, Lord,
   and now we invite you
   to the entire marriage
   and all that distance
   we shall be travelling together.

I'm approaching my birthday –
   one of those significant ones –
and I thought I'd put some time aside
   to think things over
   in your company, Lord.

I want to face questions
   like, 'What have I done
   with my life so far?'
   and, 'Where do I need things
   to be different?'

So shall we face them together?

O my God,
  I feel so excited
  and I want to share it
  with you.

What I thought was
  completely beyond my reach
  I have achieved.

Now that I've passed,
  all the hard work
  seems worthwhile.

But I can hardly believe
  it's really happened.

Thank you, my God,
  for all your love and support.

What next?

It's not that long, Lord,
   before I retire,
   and I want to talk over with you
   how best to prepare
   and how best to use that time.

Please guide me in all
   the important decisions,
   show me to any doors
   you want me to open,
   and, above all,
   make my life fruitful
   both now, and through my retirement.

TIME PASSES

Years ago, my God, life seemed
  a lengthy, lasting affair.

But suddenly, it's all
  a lot shorter,
  rushing past at breakneck speed,
  and I'm scared
  of it going to waste.

Not that I want to
  cram it to breaking point.

It's more a case of
  making some progress
  in things like wisdom,
  or conquering my weaknesses
  or just loving a bit more rigorously.

Take the rest of my lifetime,
  God of my making,
  and let your will
  be done in me.

The mirror may confirm
   my birth certificate, Lord,
   but inside
   I am as much me
   as I always was
   and want to thank you
   for making me this way!

So, Lord, it is time
    to adjust
    to these restrictions
    my body is imposing
    as it ages.

I've been angry with it
    long enough.

Help me, Lord,
    to learn to be fond of it again,
    and look at the things
    I can still do,
    instead of the things I can't.

I realised today, Lord,
    that I've moved on
    a generation.

It happened so gradually
    that I hardly noticed,
    and it feels a bit like
    getting used to new shoes.

As I get older
    it is comforting to know
    that you love all of me,
    and your love is not in the least affected
    by my age or looks
    or health or capabilities.

I've been dipping into
   memories, Lord God,
   and thinking
   how much
   the world has changed
   since I was young.

And so many of those
   I knew and loved
   are no longer here.

It frightens me a little
   to think of the future.

I can't bear the thought
   of losing the independence
   I have always enjoyed.

Be with me every step of the way,
   whatever the journey ahead.

I realise we all have to die.

It's not so much
    the dying I dread, Lord;
    it's the last stages of the journey.

It's the leave-taking,
    the ebbing of life,
    the body fighting to live.

These things unnerve me.

Loving God,
    calm my fears
    and give me the courage
    to face this final journey
    into new life.